Alfred's

INSTRUMENTAL

CD+
INSIDE

PLAY-ALONG

Trombone

ACCENT ON ACHIEVEMENT

POP, ROCK, AND MOVIE

INSTRUMENTAL SOLOS

Selected and Edited by John O'Reilly

Arranged by Bill Galliford and Ethan Neuburg
Recordings Produced by Dan Warner, Doug Emery and Lee Levin

© 2016 Alfred Music
All Rights Reserved. Printed in USA.

ISBN-10: 1-4706-3515-1
ISBN-13: 978-1-4706-3515-2

Contents

ROAR

Words and Music by
KATY PERRY, BONNIE McKEE,
MAX MARTIN, LUKASZ GOTTWALD
and HENRY WALTER

Track 2: Demo
Track 3: Play-Along

WE ARE YOUNG

Track 4: Demo
Track 5: Play-Along

Words and Music by
NATE RUESS, JEFF BHASKER,
ANDREW DOST and JACK ANTONOFF

We Are Young - 2 - 1

Track 6: Demo
Track 7: Play-Along

I SEE FIRE

Words and Music by
ED SHEERAN

I See Fire - 2 - 1

35 *Bridge:*

43 *Chorus:*

f

1.

2.

mp

JUST GIVE ME A REASON

Words and Music by
NATE RUESS, ALECIA MOORE
and JEFF BHASKER

Just Give Me a Reason - 2 - 1

Track 10: Demo
Track 11: Play-Along

FIREWORK

Words and Music by
KATY PERRY, MIKKEL ERIKSEN,
TOR ERIK HERMANSEN, SANDY WILHELM
and ESTER DEAN

Firework - 2 - 1

JUST THE WAY YOU ARE (AMAZING)

Track 12: Demo
Track 13: Play-Along

Words and Music by
KHALIL WALTON, PETER HERNANDEZ,
PHILIP LAWRENCE, ARI LEVINE
and KHARI CAIN

Just the Way You Are (Amazing) - 2 - 1

Track 14: Demo
Track 15: Play-Along

HOME

Words and Music by
DREW PEARSON and GREG HOLDEN

Home - 2 - 1

Track 16: Demo
Track 17: Play-Along

DAYLIGHT

Words and Music by
SAM MARTIN, MASON LEVY,
ADAM LEVINE and MAX MARTIN

Moderate rock (♩ = 120)

Daylight - 2 - 1

GIRL ON FIRE

Track 18: Demo
Track 19: Play-Along

Words and Music by
BILLY SQUIER, JEFFREY BHAKSER,
ALICIA KEYS and SALAAM REMI

Moderate rock (♩ = 92)

Girl on Fire - 2 - 1

Track 20: Demo
Track 21: Play-Along

BEST DAY OF MY LIFE

Words and Music by
ZACHARY BARNETT, JAMES ADAM SHELLEY,
MATTHEW SANCHEZ, DAVID RUBLIN,
SHEP GOODMAN and AARON ACCETTA

Best Day of My Life - 2 - 1

Track 22: Demo
Track 23: Play-Along

BEST SONG EVER

Words and Music by
EDWARD DREWETT, WAYNE HECTOR,
JULIAN BUNETTA and JOHN RYAN

Moderate dance rock (♩ = 118)

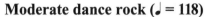

Best Song Ever - 2 - 1

DANCING QUEEN

Words and Music by
BENNY ANDERSSON, STIG ANDERSON
and BJORN ULVAEUS

Moderate disco beat ♩ = 102

Dancing Queen - 2 - 1

Dancing Queen - 2 - 2

MANY MEETINGS

(from *The Lord of the Rings: The Fellowship of the Ring*)

Music by
HOWARD SHORE

Track 28: Demo
Track 29: Play-Along

BOTH SIDES, NOW

Words and Music by
JONI MITCHELL

poco rit.

Track 30: Demo
Track 31: Play-Along

SPIRIT IN THE SKY

Words and Music by
NORMAN GREENBAUM

Moderate blues shuffle (♩ = 128)

Spirit in the Sky - 2 - 1

Track 32: Demo
Track 33: Play-Along

GONNA FLY NOW
(Theme from *Rocky*)

Words and Music by
BILL CONTI, AYN ROBBINS
and CAROL CONNORS

Moderately ♩ = 96

Gonna Fly Now - 2 - 1

Track 34: Demo
Track 35: Play-Along

NEED YOU NOW

Words and Music by
DAVE HAYWOOD, CHARLES KELLEY,
HILLARY SCOTT and JOSH KEAR

Moderately (♩ = 108)

Chorus:

Need You Now - 2 - 1

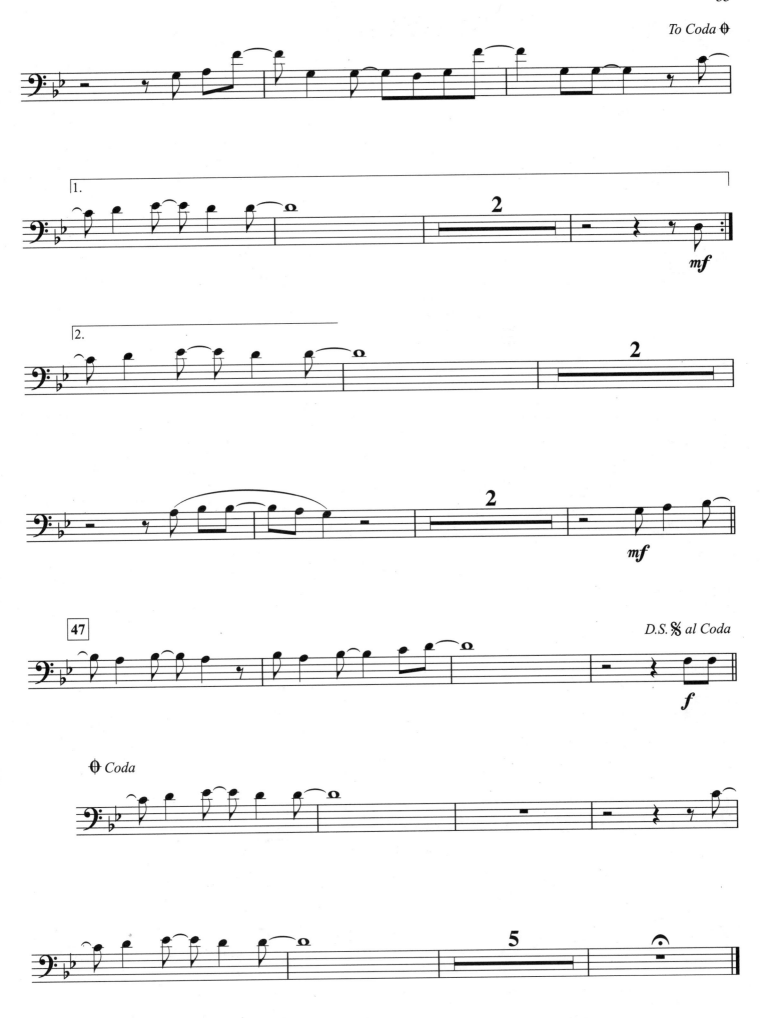

YOU RAISE ME UP

Words and Music by
ROLF LOVLAND and
BRENDAN GRAHAM

STATUES

(from *Harry Potter and the Deathly Hallows, Part 2*)

Track 38: Demo
Track 39: Play-Along

By
ALEXANDRE DESPLAT

Moderately, with movement (♩ = 132)

Track 40: Demo
Track 41: Play-Along

OVER THE RAINBOW
(from *The Wizard of Oz*)

Lyric by
E.Y. HARBURG

Music by
HAROLD ARLEN

MAY THE FORCE BE WITH YOU

(from *Star Wars Episode IV: A New Hope*)

Track 42: Demo
Track 43: Play-Along

Music by
JOHN WILLIAMS

Track 44: Demo
Track 45: Play-Along

GRENADE

Words and Music by
CLAUDE KELLY, BRODY BROWN,
PHILIP LAWRENCE, ARI LEVINE,
ANDREW WYATT and BRUNO MARS

Moderately (♩ = 112)

Grenade - 2 - 1

Track 46: Demo
Track 47: Play-Along

From Walt Disney's Frozen

LET IT GO

Music and Lyrics by
KRISTEN ANDERSON-LOPEZ
and ROBERT LOPEZ

Let It Go - 3 - 1

42

*C♭ = B

STAR WARS

(Main Theme)
(from *Star Wars Episode IV: A New Hope*)

Music by
JOHN WILLIAMS

Track 48: Demo
Track 49: Play-Along

Track 50: Demo
Track 51: Play-Along

DON'T STOP BELIEVIN'

Words and Music by
JONATHAN CAIN, NEAL SCHON
and STEVE PERRY

Moderate rock (♩ = 120)

Don't Stop Believin' - 2 - 1

Don't Stop Believin' - 2 - 2

Track 52: Demo
Track 53: Play-Along

RAIDERS MARCH
(from *Raiders of the Lost Ark*)

Music by
JOHN WILLIAMS

March (♩ = 126)

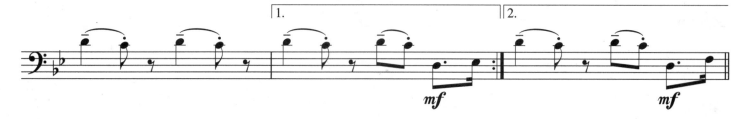

Raiders March - 2 - 1

Raiders March - 2 - 2

HEDWIG'S THEME

(from *Harry Potter and the Sorcerer's Stone*)

Music by
JOHN WILLIAMS